NYMPH-OLEPSY

NYMPH-OLEPSY

POEMS BY RODGER KAMENETZ

DRYAD PRESS
Washington, D.C. & San Francisco

Acknowledgements
Poems in this book have previously appeared in the following magazines and anthologies. The author is grateful for permission to reprint them here. ''A Construction of Clouds,'' ''Fountains,'' ''Nympholepsy,'' ''Southern Crescent'' in *Shenandoah*; ''Experimental Crossing,'' ''Elegy with Dandelions'' in *Southern Review*; ''Mallarmé in Tournon'' in *Antioch Review*; ''Alleged Memory Drops,'' ''Errors in Translation'' in *Mississippi Review*; ''Biograph'' in *Carolina Quarterly*; ''Christopher Magisto'' in *The Ardis Anthology of New American Poetry*; ''A Basic Geography'' in *Paris-Atlantic*; ''Counting Stars'' in *Maryland English Journal*; ''The Apartment Manager'' in *Poetry Now*; ''Changing Names'' in *Gargoyle*; ''Victims'' in *The Journal of Art Manufacture and Poetry (London)*; ''Lullaby'' in *Hanging Loose*; ''American Express'' in *Telephone*; ''Garden of Eden'' in *Poet Lore*; ''Cocky Amateurs'' in *City Paper*; ''Incredible Luck'' in *Abraxas*.

This project is supported by a grant from the National Endowment for the Arts, a Federal agency.

LIBRARY OF CONGRESS CATALOGING IN PUBLICATION DATA
Kamenetz, Rodger, 1950
   Nympholepsy: poems.
         I. Title   II.
PS 3561.A417ZN9   1985   811'.54   84-24677
ISBN 0-931848-66-0   ;
ISBN 0-931848-67-9 (pbk.)

DRYAD PRESS
15 Sherman Avenue
Takoma Park, Maryland 20912

P.O. Box 2916 Presidio
San Francisco, California 94123

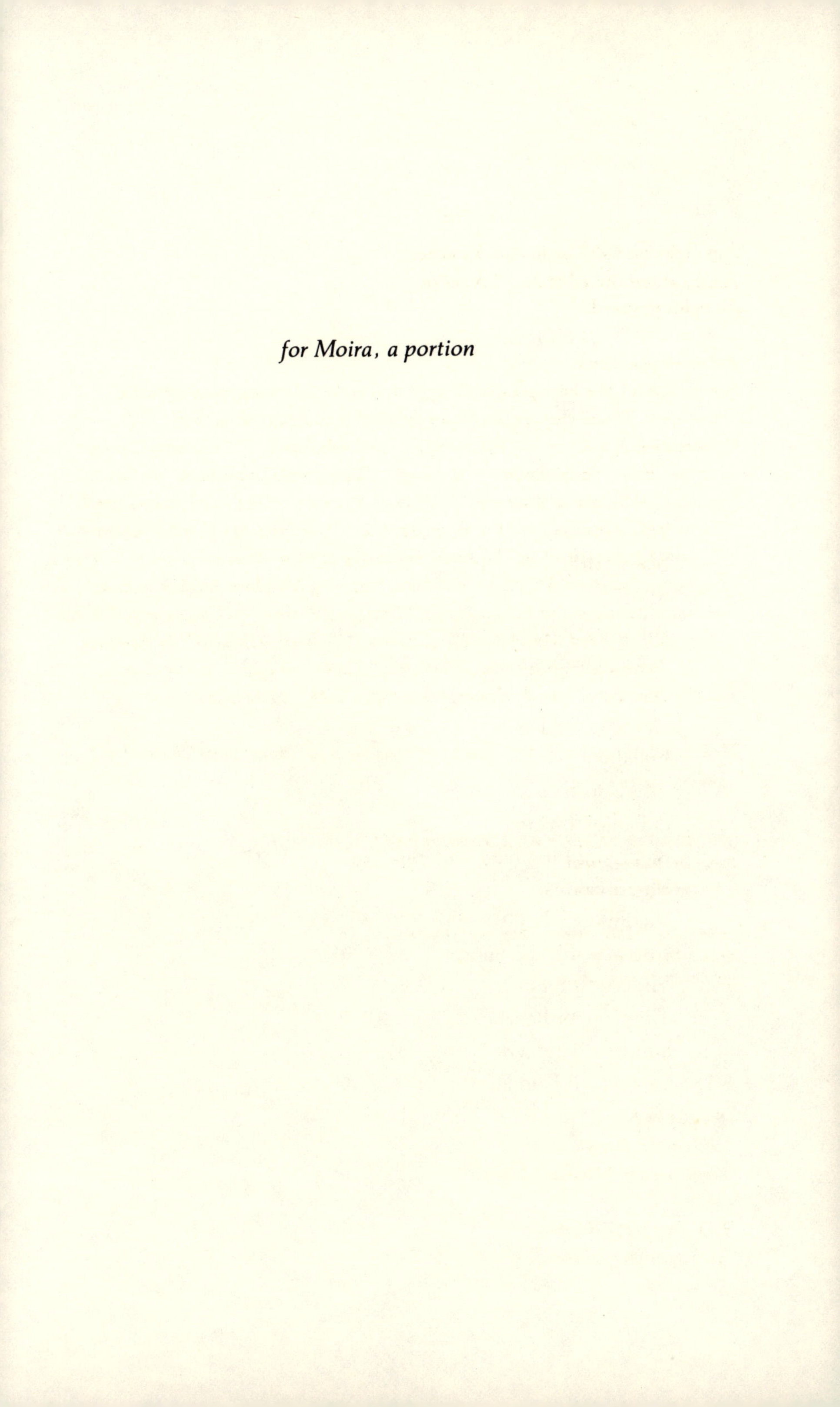

for Moira, a portion

Contents

nympholepsy (nimfolepsi). 1775. A state of rapture supposed to be
inspired in men by nymphs; hence, an ecstasy or frenzy, esp. that caused
by desire of the unattainable.

If every man had exactly what he wanted
he would be no better off than he is now.—Herakleitos

I. NYMPHOLEPSY

Nympholepsy

I had the idea of writing a poem
in which things begin very quietly
low key, musicians unpacking
their instruments, a violinist
carefully lifts her violin from its case
an oboist assembles his oboe.
Then tapping sounds, shuffling, coughs,
a janitor walks by humming a tune
the concertmaster swiftly crosses the stage
someone scrapes the floor with a chair.

I see a blonde straddle a cello,
her face creamy but flushed.
She rocks back and forth
with the instrument between her legs,
the Mozart is redundant.
In ''real life'' a telephone operator
from Ottawa I'd met at a disco.
I thought I was too good for her
but now, eyes closed, intent on the music
she ignores me, her face
is a bright cloud.

Her gown falls away and I see
intelligence, purity, wisdom embodied.
Behind her left ear, a mole
stained dark purple like a floret
of Queen-Anne's-lace in a meadow
overtaken by waves of flowers.
''How did you get here?'' I ask.

—By reading your poetry, reading
through it until I reached
the other side, where I found you,
blinking...

Fountains

for Moira

In the cities you find them.
They are quite often ugly
bronze gone pasty green, black streaks
disfiguring the faces.
Or someone has spray-painted
a slogan or a name—still
they call you. On the hot days
practically drag you out
of your way and into their
quiet zone of influence.
You feel the coolness as
a declivity, a well
among the swirling heat waves.

In winter they turn them off
desolation, fear of freezing.
You are not invited but
still you seek the empty space
where the fountain should be and
replenish it. The lack of
water corresponds to your
love of perfection, your thirst.
Call it solitude, call it
refusal to work things out—
even if you want nothing
you want it so that no one
can take it away from you.

I suppose I believe that
somewhere, even in winter
there may be water flowing.
It may take a shock to get

it going, or a pump, or
just believing that it's there.
I know when I get thirsty
I want the water to fill
a space in me I can't reach
myself. It's this sensation
that makes drinking water seem
like making love, like reaching
a simple understanding.

The old timers search for water
with a forked stick or they smell
it and you can smell water
sometimes, heavy in the air
before a storm or green and
lush standing in a puddle
where mosquitoes like to breed
but water that must be searched
for has to be fresh. That's why
they drill for days on the firm
ground that rests on water. There
are veins of gold, but the veins
of water deserve more faith.

The Orange Rug

Dropped like a raw egg
on the carefully stained walnut floor
fire orange as though something wild
had burst inside my mother's heart
some debate she'd lost with her husband,
reason, had splashed this out
alien, shaggy, a dying star
so when you walked into the house
you'd crossed a galaxy.
The suburbs fused in this hot hole
my mother's angry eye.

Her doomed mop patrolled close behind
for every footstep left its mark
on the highly susceptible floor
sensitive to the finest irritations.

Exquisitely stoned I quivered there
while the Beatles strummed my bones.
My body dilated
like a slit in a tiger's eye.

I was a son of a bitch
who was more than a bitch
called out on the carpet
from then until now, one rug
one thread genetically tangled
and vibrant in the soft white light
of the shoji screen that slid open
to a view of our neighbor
in her bathrobe. A cigarette
dangled from her misshapen lip
sprinkling grey ash on her bosom
and revealing the terrible
lack of majesty in our lives.

Cocky Amateurs

Our lips were ambulances
speeding towards the coast
cocky amateurs on to a fire
that would make arsonists rich.

And your languid body poured
out of your clothes bra
unhooked and breasts
soft in the breeze.

The danger of sleeping under cocos
made sex realistic like in army
films or how you might catch diseases
if you were lucky.

And didn't the night shush
the old ladies while you were
gliding to the radio lost
in the palms?

Moonlight blanches the sheets.
Like hearts of celery buried alive
we take on flavor in the dark.
Perhaps in secrecy growing
underground our roots have touched.

The Chastening

In a language all errors
you whisper to her while
a shout in the street flares
like a bandana of flame
against the dark walls.

If you gave her a charm
all gold, in the shape
of a hand, would it
cure her of your touch?

Or a crude angel
eyes cut like X's
its damaged wings of tin
a poor offering?

The moths whirl
in the searchlight beam
for hours, they have
nothing else to live for
and then the light
switches off. They must
scatter and fail.

Their lives are tiny
but inside each
is a particle of darkness

else they would not be
attracted to flame.

Black Girl

(a translation of Mallarmé's ''Une Negresse'')

A black girl stirred by the devil himself
Licks her lips over a sad girl's new fruit
That show like criminals beneath her torn dress.
The black glutton gets ready for something cute.

She juggles on her belly two happy nipples
And so high there's no way to grab her
She darts the vague shock of button boots
Like a tongue unschooled in pleasure.

To the quivering nakedness of a gazelle
She plays a dark elephant gone wild
Sprawls on her back, adoring herself
Laughing with naive teeth at the child.

And between her legs where her victim hides
Lifting a black flap beneath the hair
The palate of a strange mouth slides
Forward, like a sea-shell, pink and pale.

Moira

    While terns bathe in the last
green light of the sun,
    mixing in the dark waters
you add and subtract

    our days. He laughs
with all joy extracted
    when he feels
his fate blow over him—

    or he may meet the woman
whose love will take away
    everything, the orange
skin crushed at his feet.

    To know himself, even
painfully, to cross over
    into darkening waters
the ferry pitching and heaving

    the waves like black hair
streaked with grey...
    Or now wandering
the streets of a Mayan town

    where all the eyes are shy
and avert themselves in tiny waves
    as he passes.
How can a man know himself?

    The authority of his pain
comes back to him
    he cannot let it go
like the bruise in his heel

it taps him at every step.
Just as a dash of sunshine
    cuts through the dark streets
lighting a young girl's cheek

    and brushing her hair
with brilliance, so he
    is struck and shines.
Whether he is moving

    or being moved.

Alleged Memory Drops

He bought the ''alleged'' memory
drops for seventy-nine cents
red dyed camphor oil in
a cheap pharmaceutical bottle
to rub on his temples
to restore memory.

These garish potions
were magic for someone
the law of the marketplace
guaranteed it.
Someone bought and believed
''alleged love drops'' ''good luck potion''
''hug me'' ''memory'' ''come hither lotion''
rubbed love drops on his fly
success oil on his wallet
and waited for money and women
to swim through an ether
in the thin summer air
lapping the sides of walls

and who could tell him
it wasn't worth trying
to remember
her hands
preserved in memory syrup
on his thigh
bathed in success oil
one lucky night
tinctured
filtered and dissolved
lost finally lost
except for the hard odor
the vial unscrewed—

American Express

In New Orleans
they stole my tape recorder
my cassettes and my carrying case.

In Tijuana
they stole my car
my books, my diaries.

And in Oaxaca
they stole everything:
my shoes, my wife, my teeth.
It was beautiful—the thoroughness...

The Apartment Manager

It's not enough to collect rents
you have to know the tricks of the trade
the little red button beneath the garbage Dispose All
the tenants accidentally shut off.
Then they call you—
screaming for a plumber
—a flick of the switch
makes you incredibly competent.

It's the little things that count
the toilet that won't flush
the sink stopped up
drain full of hair.

Once a bathtub filled
overnight with sewage
that crept out of the drain and slid
back and forth across the porcelain tub
in long black snakes
while the tenant wept softly
in her bedroom.

Garden of Eden

Don't make it known
that is,
fat and forgettable.

Better to keep it
under moss

Always there
after a drink
and ready

Until a nerve splashes
along a blue stem
waking a dark bloom

its delicate bud folded
more secret
than an ear.

Lullaby

You put me to sleep, you really do.
Your confessions, your demands.
The clack clack clack of your voice
is a mechanism.
A stroke of the clock and tick
everything goes sleep.

Your words my words
that you suffer that I don't.
Blah.
Blah blah.
The moon
in my window.
Your wonderful hands
in my hair
put me to sleep.

The Couch

You are dead tired on the couch after quitting, too tired to breathe
too tired to yearn: this sweaty word ''yearn.''
I want to yearn for you out of context
of your life or mine.
This disruption we are constantly effecting
must be yearning in some form
and our disaffection for everything obvious—
I mean our hatred of the world—
must be a form of yearning too
though a yearning back, probably
to a previous blissful state
where we were cheated of something
the glow of childhood I think.

I want to be with you
always yearning together on the same path.
I want you crowding me
making me a little less safe
a little more sudden.

A Ball of Twine

''Poetry is news that stays new''
        Who knows?
Impractical knowledge passes
        Thought passes through thought
Your brain is a sky
Your thoughts are
                        a string
                Smoke rushes in a swirl of twine

What's between you and me
                                could get unstrung
        We must be careful unwinding
    to see the scene
                        a cloud a cloud
            and a blue burnished blue
            a child and a kite
                                and a ball of twine
            a hill and a hill and a hill
                                nothing clever
            and into the thin ''I-am-him'' enters
                                        a twin
your careless you
                all splayed and spliced
                haloed toothpicks of light
                                    your nimbus
            your cumulo-nimbus   your cloud
                and cloud cover

Pull up your cover over my chin
                            be my twin
                and twine your leg
                            with mine

Baltimore Plumbing and Heating

Would you call that love
the feeling you ''get'' I mean
                        like a check in the mail
     just how you feel
                        lines of sunlight
     slashing your face
                        into slats of hearty glowing flesh

The cat flips over with hind legs spread
                                   and licks her ass
I'd call that lovely
                   what would you call it?

Whenever we are called
                       we better have an answer
     like next month is entirely weightless
     until it is used
by two species of American
          the bill-collectors
                        & the bill-payers
and we're the third party
                        we've had this month
          we're called bill-evaders
                             if we're called at all

The cat is hungry and wants to eat
     long slow arms wrap funny chests

let's drop the neutron-erotic bomb
     and make love safe in our time!
but it's never safe, is it?
          & it's called the neurotic bomb, isn't it?
          & the cat must be fed
          the bills must be paid

Mr. Breakfast

When the stars get witty
    stellar gas wisecracks
lightning over birth-marked planets
Exploding sunshine! eternity-in-a-minute!
    and how 'd you like your eggs?
    All full of hydrogen,
            the elementary yellow
        inside the wobbling light
yoking
        my way of pronouncing *sunshine*
to the weather outside all golden
    flecked like greasespots on scrambled eggs
while slim rivers of bacon slog
    across the white china plate
                                like folk songs
''Of course! It 's morning! Buds open!
        Leaves open! Bakeries open!''
It 's breakfast, time to break open
    the smiles, the yolks, the morning glory

Victims

They found him with an X
hacked into his back
with an axe
with eggs in his hands
and an apron round his belly.

And they found her
in the back of the shop
the hilt of a knife
at the heel of her skull
and her eyes gone purple.

And they found him
hanging in the closet
near a cashmere coat.

And they found her trampled
at the bottom of the boat
blood and spittle
on her ears and throat.

And they found him
lying in an alley
a hole in his head
the size of a wallet.

And they found her
stricken in church
face white as snow
sleeping so soundly
no one had noticed.

Just Missing the Sunset

Off in the west behind
the telephone wires
sunset roughens the sky.

I want to see it whole
and head towards the lake
but it is cold and east.

Broken wine bottles dumped
from the overpass make
shore-walking difficult.

Just earlier I might
have seen the cypress hung
with windy cotton—cranes.

The Moth Elegy

(1)

I gather my task
    is to hover
knowing a blunt touch
would powder the air

always looking for the light
    coming to light
only on the cold white wall

(2)

Maybe you didn't notice at first
the way it was careful to hug
the lip of a shadow, that it
didn't move and when it did,
you felt the intruder as if
a part of your body, a lip
an eyebrow, had reclaimed
its independence and growing
wings gone off on its own

(3)

Greedy antlered swiveling sucking
    moth mouths

hard to pronounce
    furry jaws
locomoting over
    whirling fuzzy light

    bright orange thing!
    in reality, genital
    of male moth

The female straddles
    bright orange thing!

If she can take him
    she can take anything
possibly new moth life
    flitting from broken casing
possibly hand
    thwacking moth possibility
    into dusty spattered wall

(4)

Dots of dusky light
    carried mothback
alternate summers and winters
    in a pattern visible
as tiny gradations
    of diffraction grating
each distinction equally precise
    each dazzling in the bravura
of the total effect

Lines of swollen print
    march over the hill
        into the valley of the binding
    where all patterns fold
their wings

(5)

Eyelids soft as moth skin
    seal sleeping dust
        tight shut

A night's dreams wait
    at lashes' edge

      to slip under
the long black obedient hairs
    parallel stitched
      tight shut

Moth wings flutter
   the twin moons
      track
   under the lids

fingertips of a blind man
feeling his way out

(6)

Caviar eyes
beam their egg-light
his hands fly up and down

Moth wings beat time
against window panes
until they break them
with the weight
of acres of dust
and carry the flailing boy
up in a sailboat

the sail, one flashing
   composite
mother of pearl
   wing

(7)

Moon- and porchlight
also stadium lights, attractors
for thousands of moth fans

glowing musical lights
that do not move
just burn
Thousands and thousands of white
angel wings clapping
    noiselessly over
        still and by now
            deserted stadium

Why not turn off the lights
and give moths a night off?

Near my porchlight
    a single black one
with very fine and lacy shawl
    of what appears to be
        lightly sprinkled and dyed
            confectioner's sugar

(8)

Above me, spread in a gown of living
multi-colored moths rising
in splendor
with a thousand tiny eyes
each plucking a scintilla of light...
the goddess

But why does she wear
a moth-beating gown?

The dictionary says nothing
yet adds:
        moth ball
            moth bean (see 'mat bean')
                moth-eaten
                    mother

The Copper Beeches

Everything okay but difficult
as the passage from north to north
the rose opens in thorn
and each day is the same
the amount of talk wasted
by our nervous exactitude
drives us into blades.

Rain soaks the ground
and floods the gardens
as mother rides into dark weather
on her mechanical bed, raised
like a throne, lit
by fluorescents.

We attend her bearing gifts
of rotting fruit and fruit flies
French mints and purses.

It is too slow
cerebellum-fig
tumor dark as plum
center ''full of garbage''
spills if needle touches.

We come to take care
but no one can carry
off her dying
too slow, relentless
and undone, a river
long as a life
we cannot lift
from its bed.

The air puffed and piled
gives way.
The guardhouse struck.
A flume of smoke.
''What was that noise?''
Wires hiss among copper beeches.

We wobble, but she
who cannot stand
is majestic, the center
of all our gravity
moving through our days
a low pressure
at the base of her brain
dark bruise ''full of garbage''
rose bloated with rain.

Southern Crescent

In memory of my mother

Do you remember my poem
''The Curve of the Earth''?
Or do you ever listen there
where every poem is an elegy
in the dark that makes reading impossible
but does allow seeing the sparks
of what all poems could be
bundles of brightness
iron wheels trail
clattering along cold rails, curving
down and south, down and south.

Slow as the freight
out my window
uncoupling in a railyard
cell by cell your body
backed into death.

Now the edge of town
is no darker
than the roadbed
you traveled:
no marker, no sign.

Unless
what I heard you say that night
was ''Grandfather''
in a little girl's voice—
was that where you were going?

Red lanterns wave the Southern Crescent
past stiff sheets of sky
tucked into the earth
four in the morning
Monroe Virginia.

I can see the ties
drop into town
converge and vanish
but then upvalley
by a trick of perspective
once again they rise:

one moving forward
another moving back
through a vanishing point.

Elegy With Dandelions

A bunch of dandelions stuck
in an urn like a yellow hand
dangling at the foot of her grave.

Cottonwood leafing, leaving spring
in the hands of the living
while the dead pluck moving shadows,

the flickering word on the wing
that deciphered says, nothing lasts—
even the bird unidentified

just a cluster of whirring
pearl and a coo until a dove
condenses out of the worry
over names and rests peacefully

among the million leaves above
the cemetery, head buried
then unveiled by the shifting leaf
and shadow: its name is mourning.

II. THE EXPERIMENTAL CROSSING

Biograph

Better to be a crow, they said
and whip through thickets
or perch high atop a pine
and caw death down
to a fat hiker in shorts.

And crows are glorious
with black jagged wings
flashing yellow corn
in their beaks
taking long mellow flights
and never dying in public.

But to drift over cities
princely and unemployed
watching clouds buckle
sloughing their preserves
like great sloppy pies...

And the food,
sea bass, striped and musky
chubbies, dark and roiling
clams, dropped from heights
or the bait some fisherman left
drying on the dock

but I am thin
for mostly I lack
the tact to stop.
At night, the wind unbuttons me.
I huddle with my wings
closed about my craw.

Mallarmé in Tournon

Nothing
Just the blue
Not a dot on the horizon
Dinner's done and the last noises
of the village have died down
I am not even tired
Today they didn't starve me with questions
or wring the last ounce of feeling from my skin
Monsieur P— even says I show ''promise''
as a schoolmaster

I have not yet shown them my queer lazy side
I am reasonably attentive to their announcements

Because I am young they expect more to come
They don't know I'm burning at night
the fabulous coal of their future
They have plans
for they arrange the desks in rows
The pupils who thread the maze
will have first chance to rearrange it
Happy permutations!
No guess who will wind up in front
Perhaps some day I will stumble into place
and success will pay me back
Until then I make only
the most obvious calculations
As I am outside the sum
I can be added on indefinitely
without effect, like a zero

Zero had to be invented
The other numbers were merely practical
apples and oxen
but zero was the truth of their predicament
the glittering varnish of their sum
And I am a zero, *hors-concours*
though I don't abide mistakes in my salary

Christopher Magisto

I work in a theater
where the magic tricks
go too slowly for the audience
until they weep or cry out.
Always fooled
by their desire to know everything
they are as cruel as they are conscious.
When they ask for the trick
I empty my sleeves.

They close their eyes
and give me their dreams
which I turn into objects
that tumble down long shafts.
In the bright sunlight
they disappear.

The house lights come on
bringing deep clarity and regret.
The audience has aged.
Old women leave the places of young mothers.
Their children have become men.

They no longer care
how I do it.

Errors in Translation

I do not remember (precisely) the bus ride
  from Puerto Escondido to Oaxaca

I do not remember sleeping on the floor
  of the Oaxaca bus station in the early
  morning waiting for hotels to open (in detail)

I do not remember the name of the hotel
  I checked in and do not want to make one up

I do not remember the name of the man
  who came into my room demanding
  to search my luggage
  but I do remember I thought he was
  the hotel manager telling me something
  about my luggage and I told him
  never mind, I have no luggage
  and he took out a gun
  and asked me to dump my knapsack now,
  ahorita

I do remember the afternoon before
  kneeling in the arbor in Puerto Escondido
  against a chalky white wall while
  Pedro or Humberto or some o
  I do not remember dumped
  an aluminum bowl full of very rich
  pine-green *mota* and ran his stubby
  fingers through it, dropping it in cascades
  to the floor, twigs and seeds
  and it seems I remember
  him saying in Spanish though the translation
  may be faulty, ''I am rich, I am rich
  I will always be rich, rich, *rico*...''

A Basic Geography

The climates, temperaments
strategies for survival
in cold and barren lands

tundra, the Lapps...

What to do
with unnecessary fact?

There is a country
where it is impolite
not to give directions

Instead the native will lie

Turn left three blocks
turn right down fictive streets
never to find the palacio

In X County, barren landscape
of lunar soil and swamp gas
a meteor shower left hundreds of white lakes
Each a perfect ellipse

Nature rarely finishes
her constructions
We expect them irregular
like ourselves, name them
headlands, finger lakes

In X County spring
the mosquitoes come out hissing
among the blueberry flowers

Months of constant travel
sleeping in small uncomfortable beds
in cheap hotels with sinks in the hallways

Many routes lead away from home
Driving east, you are limited by the sea
Driving west, a feeling of expansion

The plain tilts up into hills

The Experimental Crossing

Tired of the old descriptions of the world
a man crosses the Mojave on foot
he is learning the map over again
from the feet up, heel and sole.

Far overhead, another man is flying
not in an airplane, but at the speed
of thought. He has learned this trick
through meditation.

But the first man belongs to the bewildered
world. He turns this way and that.
He is not too proud to ask directions.
He is looking for a mountain.

He sees it, finally, tangent to himself
a giant body, meaning in its folds,
an erect idea forced against
abutting canvases: the blank earth

the white sky. All mountains are
like prayers lifted with great force
from a dry and placid earth.
He hoists his body up the path

the landscape unwinds. Nothing
blocks his way but dry air.
His shoulders lift level
with the shoulders of the mountains.

The desert below seems to breathe.
His shoes, fallen apart. His clothes
worn out. The sky is a shout
diminishing to a whisper.

The edge of a rainbow bleeds into a
permanent illustration of the vagueness
of violet, the transitory red.
He is no longer in a desert.

He is standing in a place where
the desert ends. Just to be on
the edge of things is violently
worth it, just to stand there

not thinking but feeling it all.
It stays with him as a destination
when this wandering learns its method
learns itself as a return. Then

the mountain is auspicious and bold,
a capital letter in the long reading
you have done, preparing for the
sanctioned moment, as when

rising out of the landscape,
the extra step taken while you
were staring at your feet—
the mountain startles you.

Text and context, mountain and day
dreamer, the clear frightening
feeling of having done this before
of having been born with this trip

in mind. Any discovery is a loss
if only of, anticipation. To return
to a discovery refreshed
is more difficult than making it

for the first time. Then it was new
and exciting, now it is old and dim
more like a memory than a perception
harder to fix in its details.

Pacing the desert, walking the desert
not exactly aware of the light
as it fades out. But when the constellations
come out with extra stars in them

you know how deeply visual your memory
must be. Trying to make connections
between all those dots, aren't the myths
simply reliable rumors, the stars

a guide for perplexed shepherds?
The pilot's myth is radar.
The truth is hardly objective either
but just takes longer to see.

Just find a mountain to stand on
and the neighboring mountains become
visible, and beyond them
oceans of rhetoric, with waves shifting

constantly in response to distant
catastrophes, so that what was plain
to all, and equally plane, is now seen
as only a small part of the picture

and the mountain itself is what
we are always discovering it to be
a redistribution of the confusion
into topes and topics,

the swirls of the desert
the dry bottoms of abandoned lakes
and seas—even the useful habitations
where a few stubborn men cling to

the edge of salt flats and
the plausibility of water.
So we go back to the old stories
as comforting norms, maps of the place

we are always getting to and isn't
the idea of maps also a furious trick
a complicating division of attention
focusing on the abstractions when the

bumps in the road are straight ahead?
There is a place that is no place
a time that is no time. No mass,
no scale, no difference. The nothing

that is something is not
a simple paradox, but a tangible
illustration of origin. It is
the mountain, detached from the earth

alone in its weight and value.
That is the idea. To get back to
the beginning, but only at the end.
And to wind up there without much

happening inside, with no expectation
certainly no disappointment. Otherwise
the trip will begin again, this time
with every direction the same

and nowhere to step but light.
For it is the tendency of all explanations
to veer away from the truth
just at the point they start getting

interesting. And the idea that there is
a truth puts mountains in our path.
To keep on explaining this is certainly
a sign of additional interference

it is a sign that the walking
has grown to be a habit, almost parallel
to the breath required, just as
the excitement in the ease of its happening

is a spur tempting the traveller beyond
exhaustion into the domain
where the metaphysical gets really interesting
since it begins to haunt flowers

rocks and trees. There the old myths
revive and the stories of mountains
talking and maidens merging into trees
are like apologies to the landscape

for having all this consciousness.
There is no single point of view
that will justify it and the silence
is convenient. Out there is

a new mountain that has always been
but until now just not noticed
nor ever so obtainable
nor ever so attractive.

A Construction of Clouds

He rises perfectly into the sky
a young god with a talent
for suffering on behalf of others.

Four hundred years stripped away
Raphael's yellow Jesus is in the pink
a Transfiguration fresh as doubt.

At his back a jumbo cloud billows
hospital white, its x-rayed brilliance
''a stunning feat of restoration''

or so the museum poster claims.
Whatever is holy evaporates, I think
weeks later as a wet sundown

paints a lawn of flies, twitching
of cow tails and horse behinds
and quotes a sky of Raphael originals

for our unvarnished Baton Rouge.
We peer into a mist that wipes the levee
like a damp rag. Will some god come

to rescue us, restore our faded daydreams
to their true colors? The sky divides
into swimming pools of silver and green.

It is an amazing weather that
builds a palace of clouds high
as the eye can climb then sends it

tumbling down like a child's blocks
with adult croaks of thunder
to punctuate the shape of things to come.

The building of clouds is on the rise
knock them down who will, the bright
flashes of their tumbling, the equal rain.

Putting Away the Toys

(1)

The small weather was pleasing.
Not everything was arrogant after all.
Cars weren't.
They seemed to spill down the hillside
like crumbs a matron brushes off her lap.

He could see from the vantage of simile
how everything big was smaller than his childhood.
The hillside lap
the cars, the crumbs
''a place for everything
and everything in its place.''

Where home met homily
he had found a small religion
involving what he saw
with what he knew.

From where he stood
nothing worth seeing
could be tucked in the hollow.
What belonged to it
was the beginning of sleep.

(2)

The metaphor moved towards its reader
like a car towards a blank wall.
There was no way to stop it
at the acceleration due to language.

He banked the car
hoping to match the curve
as it bent away from him
constantly testing
his steering power.

Minute adjustments of the wheel
below the level of meaning
woke the reader just before the crash
to ask what exactly
he was driving at.

(3)

The snow settles on a ski slope.
Somehow the Ford has gotten to the top of it
and ''somehow'' is partly to blame.
Clouds of thick snow
block driveways, freeze wipers
occlude windshields, white, white
white as paper on which are written
inevitable cliches, ruined farmhouses
with sad broken boards.

''Meanwhile'' the Ford is skidding
down the slope, wheels locked
and the driver to blame.
He has lost control
of his vehicle
and is slamming up
against years of indecision
glassy walls of snow.

Yachting Charleston Harbor

Between shrimp, the belle of the boat
told me, ''Baltimore? I lost my sunglasses
in your niggertown once
dirty gas station...''

That does it: I speed out of Charleston
past the last gas up a dark
flat road between two swamps.
I have to piss, the gauge ticks empty
Exxon Exxon Exxon dark dark dark.
Finally I squeeze between a rusted pump
and a scarred grey door, step out
and tap, it swings wide and loud
on a worn pool table, stark bulb
a black man about to shoot, another
leathery face sips a Red and White.
I know anything could happen, no gas
bladder could burst, they might want
my neck, I wouldn't blame them.
''Fill it?'' and he says okay, slow
limps to the Ford while I decide
to hold it no use pressing my luck.

Incredible Luck

Incredible luck catching crabs
one after the other, fast
as I can empty the pots
three at a time grabbing
at the bait: thick meaty
grandma crabs shot with orange
roe and granddad crabs
eyes suspicious
on their stalks, claws snapping
at my slightest move.
Into the bucket they go
mean as hell and full of white
succulent meat with a hint
of blue sky in it, and there's
one more at the shore, attracted
no doubt by the sound of
his brothers splashing in the pot—
with one easy swoop
I net him too.

Beside my foot, the bait:
fishheads in the sun
soaked in hot fish blood
bubbling and stinking.

Eat 'em fast and eat 'em hot.
Don't throw a dead one in the pot.
Watch the salt sizzle
on their shells, and their death
twitches as the hot steam
hits them from underneath.
Don't eat the gills or devil
as they call it, as if anyone

would chew wormy feathers
but that white spring popping
out of the mustard soup
is quite tasty guts.

They eat garbage, jellyfish
young oysters, other crabs.
I caught an old granddad
in the pot, his harsh claws
stuck into a baby
underneath; mating, the male
carries the female like that.
They always move sideways
so tug sharp
and they'll stall
in the webbing.

My father'd bring home crabs
on hot summer nights and
I'd get out of bed in my underwear
and eat my share on THE SUN
spread out in sections to catch
the yellow juice, black pepper
and sunburnt shells, my mouth
and fingers burning, only
the calm white meat
to cool them off.

Changing Names

for Andrei Codrescu

I hereby change my name
from Rodger Kamenetz
to fill in the blank.
What's in a name?
Nothing more than
you put into it.
The roses in my name
have all wilted
but the touch of Celia's breath
would revive
them at once.

Who is Celia?
Who is Laura?
Who is Beatrice?
Who is Sylvia
that all the swains do commend her?
We make up names
to save innocent girls
from our drunken praise
so they may marry
rich men, not poets
and have many servants
one of whom, the maid
will find, locked
in a secret diary
the secret poems
addressed to the secret lady
with the secret name
and the secret number
of kisses, thirty thousand
all in a row
from Catullus to Petrarch to now.

I 'll change my name
to something, anything
but Rodger Kamenetz.
My name 's odd conjunction
splays me across time—Rodger,
the Celtic warrior,
he who carries a mighty spear
in the midst of battle—
okay, at least it 's not Dick
or Peter but the resonance
is close: I see a drunken
hairy brute with a spear
as long as a laundry pole
and thick as a baseball bat
haft set in mud
his heels have dug
a jug of mead half-tipped
at his side and arrows
mudballs, rocks and stones
thick in the air.
One meaty hand fingers
forelock and beer-soaked
beard: Rodger!

Then there 's Kamenetz
Ellis Island wisecrack.
Kamenetz: a name that roars
like thunder across the bay...
No, Kamenetz, a name so hard
to pronounce and easy to misspell
tangled in miles of cable
twisted through coves of ears
punched into guts of demented
computers and spat out:
Kavanet
Kabinets
Kamenetty

Kamentz
Ka-menn-etz
Kameneta
Kamentez
Kramentz
Kramenetz
Kanenetz
Kastanets
Kostalenetz
Katzenstein
Kamenhammer
Katzenjammer

Really, it's not even Kamenetz
but Kam-yen-yetz, the Russian e
greased by adding a sliding y
or so three big bears of Russian
bibliographers told me
at the Columbia Library
Slavic section linking
arms on their way
to the union meeting
singing the Internationale,
they hailed me, ''Come
tovarisch Kam-yen-yetz!''

Cities of grim slaughter.
I mean Kamenetzes, little towns
in Poland, Latvia, the Ukraine
cramped shtetls.
Kamenetz from Russian kamen
meaning stone and etz
makes it little, little stones
(and Rodger, a mighty spear)
mismatch of sexual equipment
but more likely a quarry town.
Kamenetz means gravel.

Cities of grim slaughter.
Jews without last names
just David son of Samuel.
It's the old story
change your name
to mark a memory
to mark a moment:
when her son was born
Sarah laughed,
Yitzhak, she laughed, Isaac
Abram became Abraham
Jacob, Israel
''he who struggles with God''
struggling still.

I hereby change my name
from Rodger Kamenetz
to idle-speculator-daydreaming-
the-new-syntax-that-will-release-
names-from-dread-history-
and-send-them-spinning-
an-echolalia-of-nonsense.

I want a name as common as dirt
a name like a mantra
as Walt Whitman hypnotized himself
chanting Walt Whitman Walt Whitman
Walt Whitman, who heard the sea
whispering death death death
and right, I hear no sea
whispering Rodger...
hear no trains clacking by
Kamenetz Kamenetz Kamenetz...
Every little breeze seems to whisper
the sound of one hand clapping

and the nightjar that keeps me
awake all summer with her lust
doesn't crack her throat on Kamenetz
but whips poor will to death.

I don't want to change my name.
I want my name changed.
I want it inhabited by force.
I want it to mean something.
I want a name to match
how dissatisfied I feel.

Oh Sammy Rosenstock
I want a name as tragic
and magical as yours
when you changed it
to Tristan Tzara
Rumanian for lost lands...
I want a change as surgical
and sure as yours
Manuel Rabinowitz
when you erased the middle west
and the middle class
with a single stroke
and became Man Ray.
And you Pablo Neruda
what was your name
before you borrowed
that dead Czech poet's?
So thoroughly you succeeded
we have lost it...
As for you, Ezra Pound
some people are just born lucky...

I hereby throw my name

into the air.
I want it digested
into something subtle
as alcohol dissolves dye
retrieving blue.
I want to cultivate
the seeds in my name.
I want to groom
that drunken lout, Rodger
and that scared immigrant, Kamenetz
and blend them into a single name
courageous and empty as a shout!

Thinking of Samuel Johnson

Tonight I am thinking of an anxious man
pacing back and forth in his study
unable to sleep. He is large and ugly
with a hydrocele hanging from his testicle
visible beneath his nightshirt. In his bony hands
he holds a large oak club to ward off
surprise attacks from James McPherson
soi-disant translator of Ossian.
His famous definition of a net
as ''anything reticulated or decussated
at equal distances with interstices
between the intersections'' left
fishermen puzzled
                    though the mind
may be the burning along a billion
interstices of a single core of meaning.
His hands trembling—there, there
just above the molten mass.

The Dictionary of Light

No one is satisfied with definitions of poetry. The dictionary of feelings was written before birth, with an analytical index like Roget's Thesaurus; shades and nuances of anger, penalty, want are spread in spectra around a single glow. In heaven, definitions flow through each other as Milton imagined angels making love, light passing through light. In heaven, all definitions are polite since there they truly find their common center. On earth, words tend to deflect from their origin: the root of black is *blanc*, meaning white. If the most elementary distinction is blurred, think of the incestuous possibilities of two antonyms already closely related by sympathetic magic, fact and fiction, fiction and fact.

The Etymology of Orchids

The habit of defining shows the sensuous origin of thinking. Just as seeing functions mentally as visualization, defining is the body's tactile sense turned brainward and then, in a grasping motion, back out into the world. Dictionaries appear late in a culture. By the time they are needed, the population is completely out of touch. To add a new word, invent a new machine: so radio, television, transistor are brought into the fold, first swearing their allegiance to the previous system of Greek and Latin roots.

The dictionary desires destruction through definition, choking the invisible filaments that hang from every viable concept—like the tender roots of certain orchids so sensitive they can draw moisture from the air. The beautiful violet orchid flowers only in the mind without definitions.

Atlantic Sundial, Knobby Whelk

A curve of articulations
inscribed in golden rectangles
each shell while perfect remembers
perfect proportions, 5:8.

In the war of all against all
the shell loses, sand strips a wall
unveiling the pearl bed chambers
of the nautilus—what is worn

does not bore, all the more since less
is more and careful invention
can restore regular marvels.
A fractured shard half-buried holds

no water or sand, yet seashells
hold someting finer, attention.
In their subtle constant angles
the shells restate and reinstate

form—what has unfolded unfolds
again obeying laws of growth
that grow beyond taxonomies
towards spirals of galaxies,

radial rotational growth.
Rainbow spine machicolations
turrets, towers, accordions
or the horn of a unicorn

abandoned stabbing sand, of strife
these are the elegant features.
Their ex-occupants, the creatures
who made them for defense, are dead.

Their remains are the skeletons
of a geometrical life
the forms, as Pythagoras said,
limit gives to the limitless.

Counting Stars

We are seeing, not believing, a world.
Our discoveries are made by science
but at the cost of legions of angels.
The light that seemed to come from within
in the medieval theory of vision
was the light of another world too bright
for us to see: we have never seen it.

We see sunlight projecting a world
we could never have really imagined
magpies and bluejays, fuchsia and violets,
who could have invented such profusion?
Seeing is not believing, cannot be.
For we believe a world until
we see it fall apart, and then we see.

The grass is a vision green as repose.
The mind admires it, the senses lie in it.
It announces a modesty to which
we have nothing to add. So silence
is golden, rivers silver, or in Leonardo
a blue world where rocks merge with the sky.
Serenity needs a place to recede.

Intelligence came to us from a star.
The eye jelled in the light and fed the brain
plump in the skull like fruit in a husk.
A hand reached for an apple and taught the brain
but first the eye saw it sparkling
and the mind formed a question so rich
it has never once been satisfied.

Counting stars can not reveal their number.
Every dark space hides a thousand stars

too far away to see. For a long time
we have been watching and yet nothing
has noticed us. Perhaps the quality
of our waiting, so stuffed with busy days
does not merit any attention

or perhaps what we are waiting for is
always with us, the way the world is if we see it
or if we close our eyes. Before us, the sky
at night seems not so much mysterious
as beyond all influence, a being
that speaks a language not of words, but of
light and darkness—and finds our voices dark.

Cover design by Susan Foster.

Nympholepsy was composed by Dan Johnson at The Writer's Center Bookworks. The typeface is Compugraphic Holland Seminar, the text paper Warren Olde Style.

RODGER KAMENETZ was born in Baltimore in 1950. He went to Yale at age 16, graduated Phi Beta Kappa at age 20, and wandered. His earliest work was influenced by Rimbaud and the young poets of the New York School. In San Francisco he met Robert Duncan, who has continued to be influential, and he has also followed in the tradition of Williams and Charles Reznikoff. *The Missing Jew*, published by Dryad Press, marked his first exploration of the Jewish tradition, an interest that has continued. *Nympholepsy*, represents another side of his activity that could be roughly characterized as a search for a mythology grounded in every day experience.

Kamenetz is currently director of the creative writing program at Louisiana State University in Baton Rouge. His poems and essays have appeared in dozens of magazines, including The Antioch Review, Shenandoah, North American Review and Grand Street.